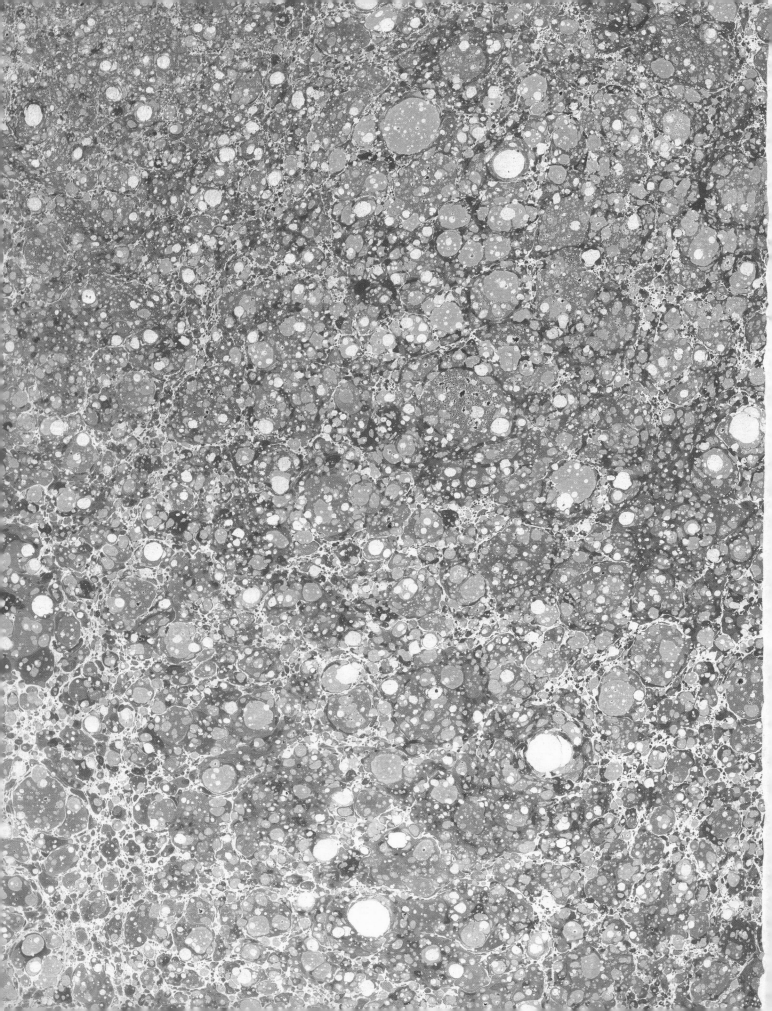

MEDIEVAL FABLES

Marie de France

MEDIEVAL FABLES

Marie de France

Translated by
JEANETTE BEER

Illustrated by
JASON CARTER

DODD, MEAD & COMPANY
NEW YORK

First published in the United States of America in 1983
by Dodd, Mead & Company, Inc.
79 Madison Avenue, New York, N.Y. 10016 by arrangement with Dragon's World Ltd.
Copyright © Dragon's World Ltd. 1981
Illustrations copyright © Bryson Graphics Ltd. 1981
Text copyright © Jeanette M. A. Beer 1981

Library of Congress Cataloging in Publication Data

Marie, de France, 12th cent.
Medieval fables.

   Selected and translated from: British Library.
Manuscript. Harleian 978.
   1. Fables, French—Translations into English.
2. Fables, English—Translations from French. I. Beer,
Jeanette M. A. II. Carter, Jason, 1940- ill.
III. Title.
PQ1494.F3E5   1983   841'.1   83-1902
ISBN 0-396-08169-X

Printed in Singapore

For Stephen and Jeremy

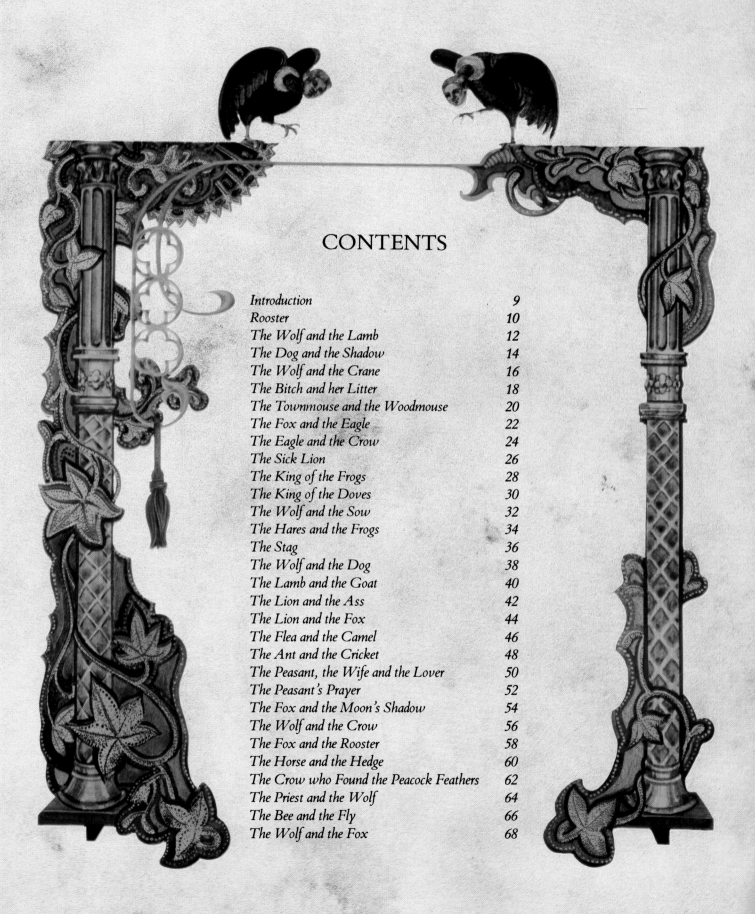

CONTENTS

INTRODUCTION

"FABLES" are stories which, as long as the world can remember, in East and West, have educated man in practical wisdom. Because fables tell their truths with animals, and because they are short, pithy and entertaining, they are always in fashion. Unrestricted to a particular time, place or civilisation, they are true without being real, useful without being tedious. They are universal.

Sometimes particular collections of fables achieve permanent success. Such are the fables told by Aesop, Phaedrus, Bidpai, and our Marie de France. The identity of this medieval Marie is a mystery that literary historians have not yet solved. We cannot interpret with certainty the clues she has given about herself in the fables. She says, for example, *Marie ai nun, si sui de France*—"My name is Marie and I am from France." Obviously she belonged to the French aristocracy who settled in England after the Norman Conquest. But *which* Marie, and *when* did she or her family go to England from France? Who was she?

Marie tells us also that she compiled her fables for love of a Count William, "the most valiant in the realm". But in spite of Marie's fervent admiration of Count William's outstanding valour, modern critics have not yet decided which Count William she could have known.

Even the literary sources of Marie's fables remain obscure. She says she made her French verse translations from a collection of fables that a certain "Alvrez" — whom she thought was King Alfred — had translated into English. Alvrez must therefore have used a Latin version of Aesop's fables for his English translation. But the manuscripts of both Alvrez and his Latin source are now lost without trace, as so many medieval authors and their works have been lost to us through the centuries.

Fortunately, particular details of time, place and author are in a sense irrelevant to fables. Fables maintain their identity always, whether borrowed by a Marie de France, a Rudyard Kipling or a Walt Disney.

The present collection contains thirty fables which were selected, transcribed and translated from the elegant little manuscript, *Harley 978*, in the British Library, London. They were chosen both for the interest of their stories and for the skill with which Marie told those stories. They are rendered in a simple prose which takes no major liberties with the originals. I have, however, shortened some of Marie's endings when they are too wordy or, even, self-contradictory. The success of a fable's "moral" has always depended upon its epigrammatic brevity. Marie was, in this respect, less skilful than her predecessors.

Regardless of any transformations in their form and substance, fables continue down through the ages. They are the repository of man's wisdom about himself, for —

these animals are men.

ROOSTER

Up on a dung-hill Rooster scratched.
He liked to scratch for food.
Up there he saw a jewel, clear and glistening.
It was a precious gem, but Rooster said:
"I wanted dinner from this place.
Instead I find a jewel.
You're no good to me!
A rich man finding you would prize you.
He would bed you down in gold.
You would look beautiful in gold . . . so dazzling!
But I, the rooster, do not want you.
You're no good to me."

A fool will leave the best and choose the worst.

THE WOLF AND THE LAMB

A wolf and a lamb stood drinking at a stream.
The wolf drank from the source,
The lamb drank further down.
The wolf, who loved a quarrel, exclaimed angrily:
"You really cause me problems!"

"How is that, my lord?"

"You mean you cannot see you've muddied up my water?
Now I cannot drink my fill.
I see I'll have to go away as thirsty as I came.
I'll die of thirst."
The lamb said: "But, my lord, *you* are the one upstream!
What *I've* drunk comes to me from *you!*"
"What!" said the wolf. "You would abuse me too?"
"That isn't my intention," said the lamb.
The wolf said: "I can see the truth of it.
Your father did just this, I do believe,
At this same stream when I was here with him
Six months ago!"

"Why blame that on me?
I wasn't even born then, I am sure!"
"So what?" said Wolf. "You're bothering me now.
You're doing what you shouldn't."
The wolf then snatched the little lamb,
And mangled him to death between his jaws.

The powerful by dishonest means confound the weak.

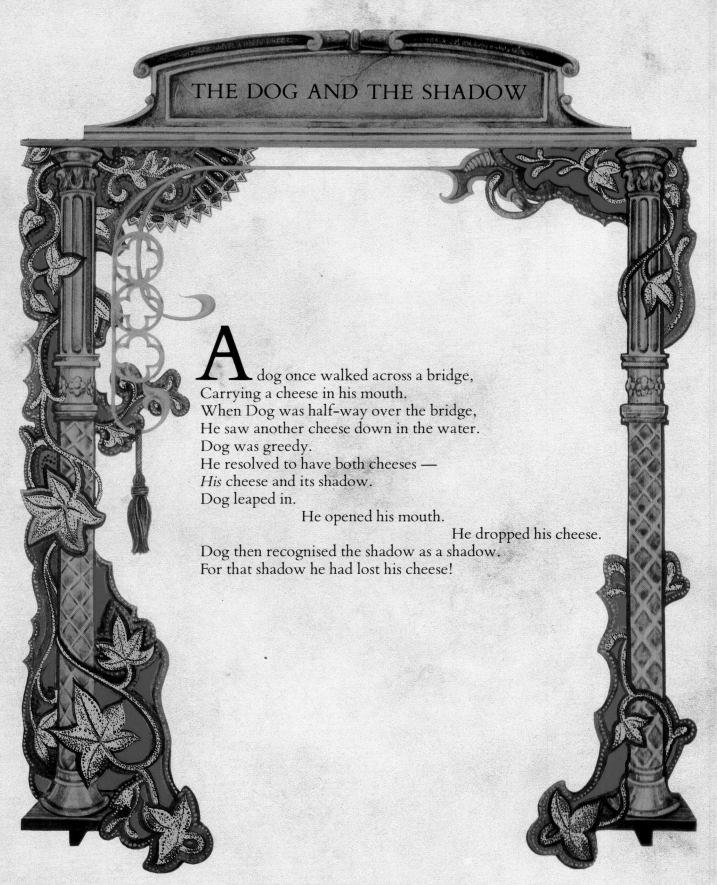

THE DOG AND THE SHADOW

A dog once walked across a bridge,
Carrying a cheese in his mouth.
When Dog was half-way over the bridge,
He saw another cheese down in the water.
Dog was greedy.
He resolved to have both cheeses —
His cheese and its shadow.
Dog leaped in.
　　　　　　　　He opened his mouth.
　　　　　　　　　　　　　　He dropped his cheese.
Dog then recognised the shadow as a shadow.
For that shadow he had lost his cheese!

To want too much may mean one loses everything.

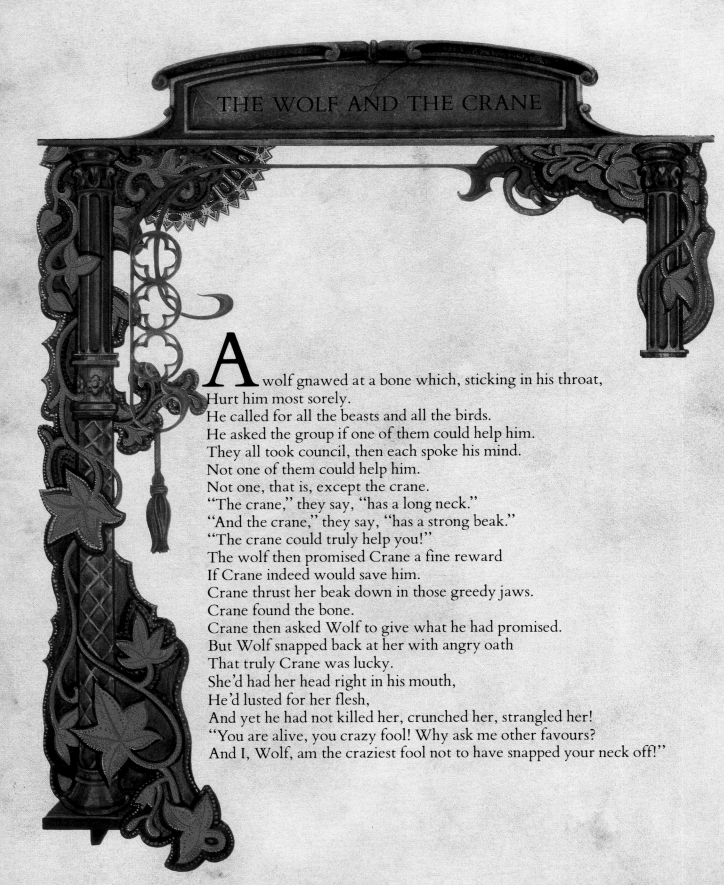

THE WOLF AND THE CRANE

A wolf gnawed at a bone which, sticking in his throat,
Hurt him most sorely.
He called for all the beasts and all the birds.
He asked the group if one of them could help him.
They all took council, then each spoke his mind.
Not one of them could help him.
Not one, that is, except the crane.
"The crane," they say, "has a long neck."
"And the crane," they say, "has a strong beak."
"The crane could truly help you!"
The wolf then promised Crane a fine reward
If Crane indeed would save him.
Crane thrust her beak down in those greedy jaws.
Crane found the bone.
Crane then asked Wolf to give what he had promised.
But Wolf snapped back at her with angry oath
That truly Crane was lucky.
She'd had her head right in his mouth,
He'd lusted for her flesh,
And yet he had not killed her, crunched her, strangled her!
"You are alive, you crazy fool! Why ask me other favours?
And I, Wolf, am the craziest fool not to have snapped your neck off!"

To serve a surly master means to cringe for very life.

16

17

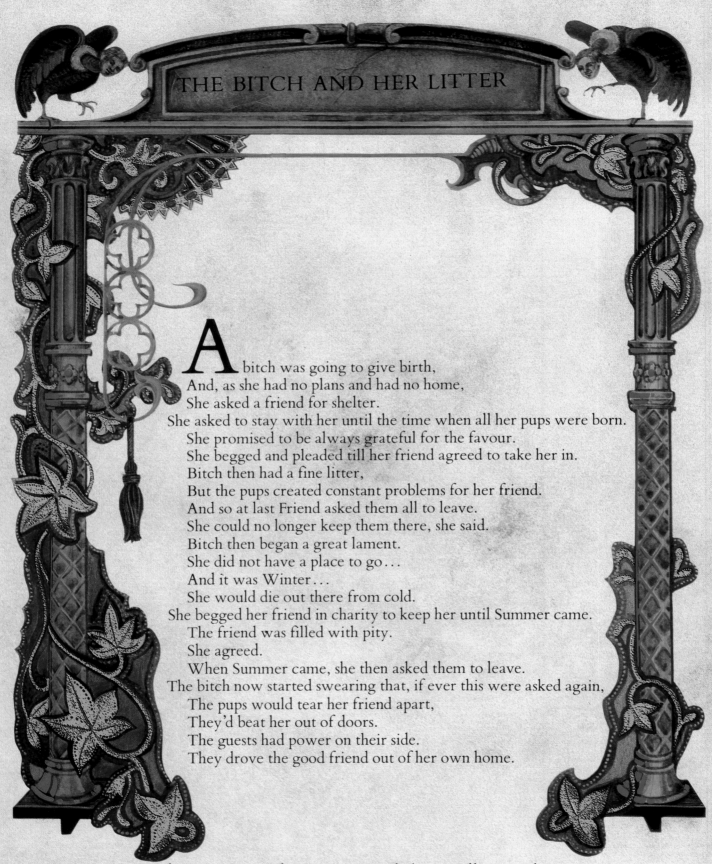

THE BITCH AND HER LITTER

A bitch was going to give birth,
And, as she had no plans and had no home,
She asked a friend for shelter.
She asked to stay with her until the time when all her pups were born.
She promised to be always grateful for the favour.
She begged and pleaded till her friend agreed to take her in.
Bitch then had a fine litter,
But the pups created constant problems for her friend.
And so at last Friend asked them all to leave.
She could no longer keep them there, she said.
Bitch then began a great lament.
She did not have a place to go...
And it was Winter...
She would die out there from cold.
She begged her friend in charity to keep her until Summer came.
The friend was filled with pity.
She agreed.
When Summer came, she then asked them to leave.
The bitch now started swearing that, if ever this were asked again,
The pups would tear her friend apart,
They'd beat her out of doors.
The guests had power on their side.
They drove the good friend out of her own home.

Welcome unworthy guests, and they will never leave you.

THE TOWNMOUSE AND THE WOODMOUSE

Night fell upon a townmouse as he travelled through the woods.
A mousehole was nearby, the well-stocked home of Woodmouse.
The townmouse asked for food and shelter there.
The woodmouse answered: "Certainly! Just see my stores of food.
If many more came knocking at my door,
You'd still have all you needed!"
The townmouse stayed a while, but then grew restive.
"What a life! I don't want to remain here any longer.
Now *you* come with *me*!
You'll have rich rooms, fine larders and fine cellars.
You'll have good food, good drink. They're yours!"
So Woodmouse in his innocence left for town.
The townmouse led him through rich rooms,
Through larders, lofts, and cellars filled with flour and honey in plenty.
He thought he was in heaven.
But while he gazed, the butlers of the house approached the door.
The mice sped into hiding.
Woodmouse was scared to death.
What was all this? He could not understand it.
Then the butlers left. The mice came back to eat.
But Woodmouse feared now for his very life.
He moped in misery.
His friend saw this and asked him kindly:
"What's your problem, Woodmouse?"
"I'm sick with fright. I'm sorry that I ever came with you.
You told me all the good things of your life without the bad.
But now I see you live in fear…of man…of cats…of birds…
And of those traps that humans set for you.
I want my woods, my peace and safety,
Not your fear-filled luxury."

A humble life in peace is better than a wealthy life in torment.

THE FOX AND THE EAGLE

A fox came out of his den
To play outside with his children.
An eagle swooped.
He carried off one little fox.
The father fox ran after them,
And shouted for his child.
The eagle would not listen,
And the father had to go back to his den.
Fox went around then gathering dry wood.
He took a burning fire-brand.
He spread wood around the oak
Where Eagle had his nest.
The eagle saw the fire's sparks…
He pleaded with the fox:
"My friend, put out the fire!
Take your child!
Or all my baby birds will surely die."

A bully is not reasonable — he is persuaded only by threats.

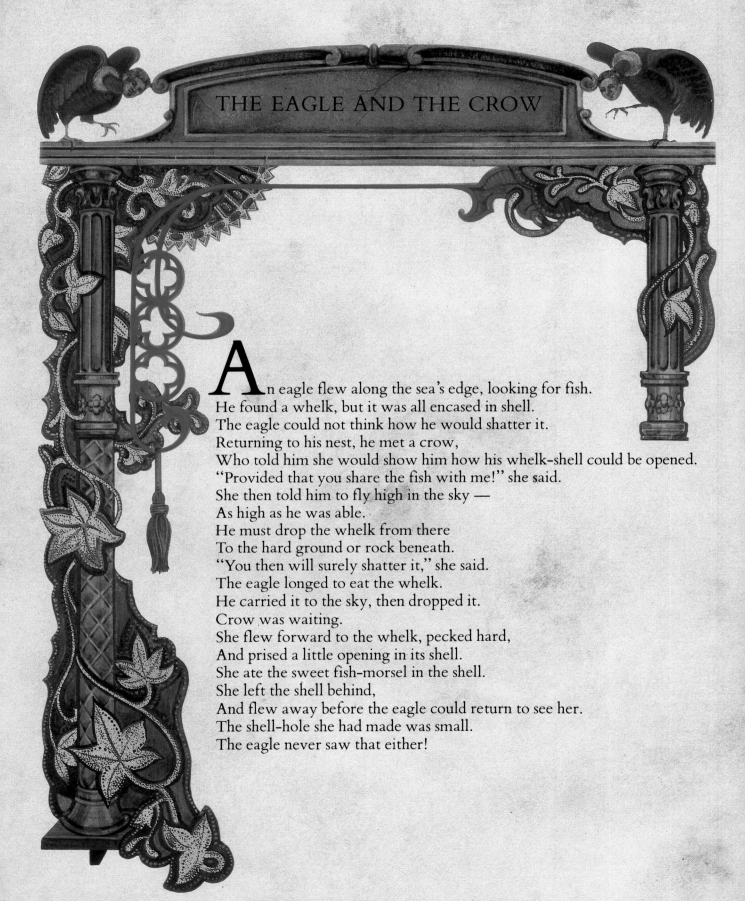

THE EAGLE AND THE CROW

An eagle flew along the sea's edge, looking for fish.
He found a whelk, but it was all encased in shell.
The eagle could not think how he would shatter it.
Returning to his nest, he met a crow,
Who told him she would show him how his whelk-shell could be opened.
"Provided that you share the fish with me!" she said.
She then told him to fly high in the sky —
As high as he was able.
He must drop the whelk from there
To the hard ground or rock beneath.
"You then will surely shatter it," she said.
The eagle longed to eat the whelk.
He carried it to the sky, then dropped it.
Crow was waiting.
She flew forward to the whelk, pecked hard,
And prised a little opening in its shell.
She ate the sweet fish-morsel in the shell.
She left the shell behind,
And flew away before the eagle could return to see her.
The shell-hole she had made was small.
The eagle never saw that either!

Beware of cunning tricksters who will steal your hard-earned gains.

THE SICK LION

An aged lion, frail and weak,
Lay a long time, not moving.
The animals assembled from his kingdom,
And all went to court to see him.
Some grieved for him.
Some hardly cared at all.
Some came there for a gift from his estate.
Most asked about his chances of recovery.
Billy-Goat butted his horns at him.
Donkey kicked him in the chest.
Fox took his turn and bit him in the ears.
The lion said: "What strange things now I see!
I well remember, in my youth and prime, all other creatures feared me.
Then they honoured me, their lord.
When I was joyful, they would laugh with me.
When I was furious, then they trembled.
But now they see me feeble, they have trampled me and spurned me.
From my foes this is less vile than from my friends.
Those I once honoured and rewarded now are thankless."

The man who loses power loses even friends.

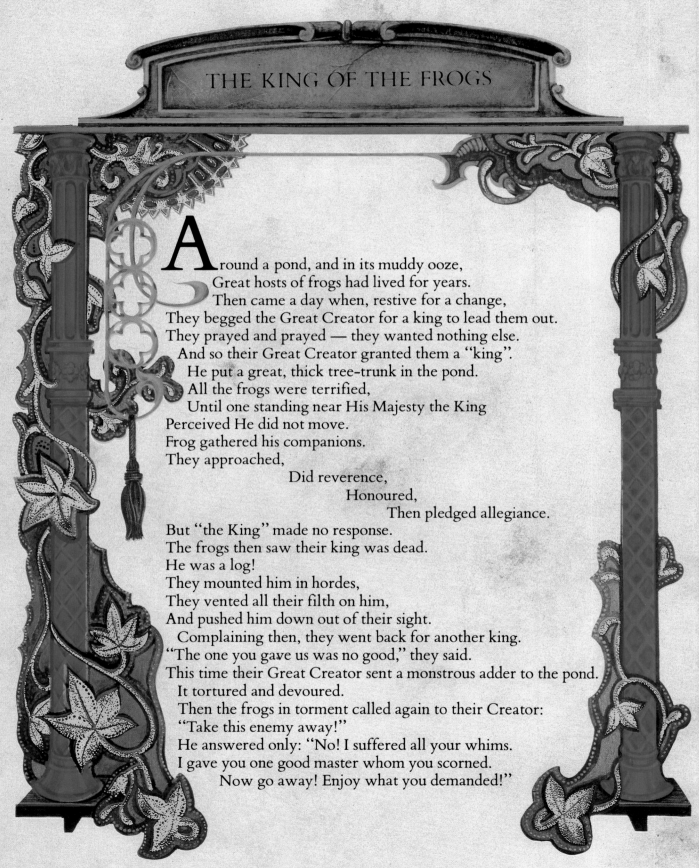

THE KING OF THE FROGS

Around a pond, and in its muddy ooze,
  Great hosts of frogs had lived for years.
    Then came a day when, restive for a change,
They begged the Great Creator for a king to lead them out.
They prayed and prayed — they wanted nothing else.
  And so their Great Creator granted them a "king".
    He put a great, thick tree-trunk in the pond.
    All the frogs were terrified,
      Until one standing near His Majesty the King
Perceived He did not move.
Frog gathered his companions.
They approached,
                Did reverence,
                    Honoured,
                        Then pledged allegiance.
But "the King" made no response.
The frogs then saw their king was dead.
He was a log!
They mounted him in hordes,
They vented all their filth on him,
And pushed him down out of their sight.
  Complaining then, they went back for another king.
"The one you gave us was no good," they said.
This time their Great Creator sent a monstrous adder to the pond.
  It tortured and devoured.
  Then the frogs in torment called again to their Creator:
"Take this enemy away!"
He answered only: "No! I suffered all your whims.
I gave you one good master whom you scorned.
      Now go away! Enjoy what you demanded!"

Good masters may not be appreciated until replaced by bad.

THE KING OF THE DOVES

The doves wanted a lord for their kingdom.
They chose a hawk because they thought that, as their king,
The hawk would harm them less.
They thought He would protect them from all enemies.
Hawk came into His kingdom, and became their lord and master.
From then on King Hawk slaughtered and devoured
Any dove who came into His presence.
"We were fools," said one, "to choose this hawk as king.
For day by day His Royal Highness kills us off.
Better to have no lord at all than to have this one!
In former times we always were on guard.
We feared only surprise attacks or ambushes.
But now we have invited Hawk among us,
He's done openly what once He did by stealth."

It is not wise to throw oneself upon a felon's mercy.

THE WOLF AND THE SOW

A prowling wolf espied a pregnant sow.
He hastened up to her and said: "God bless you!
May you soon give birth!"
(His reason was, of course, his hunger for Sow's juicy piglets.)
The sow replied to him most shrewdly,
For she said: "Good sir, how could I hurry
While I see you by my side?
As long as you are there I cannot have them.
Surely you understand the situation.
When we females are about to have our children,
Innate modesty prevents our being touched or handled by a nearby man."
The wolf then went away from her and hid —
He longed for piglets.
The sow also went away.
Her ruse had saved her.

Females must guard their children with their lives.

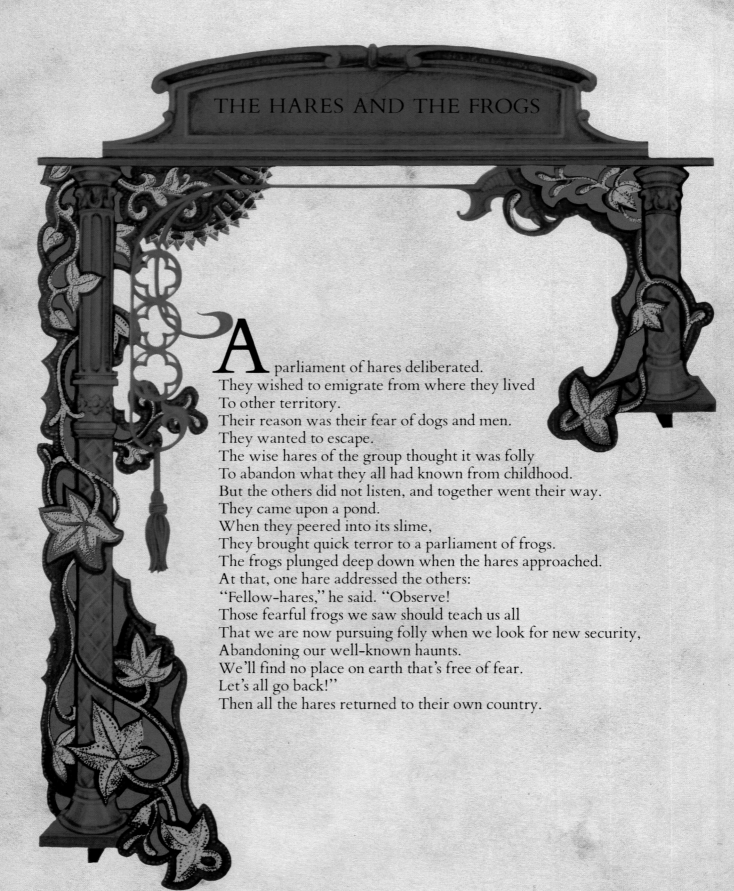

THE HARES AND THE FROGS

A parliament of hares deliberated.
They wished to emigrate from where they lived
To other territory.
Their reason was their fear of dogs and men.
They wanted to escape.
The wise hares of the group thought it was folly
To abandon what they all had known from childhood.
But the others did not listen, and together went their way.
They came upon a pond.
When they peered into its slime,
They brought quick terror to a parliament of frogs.
The frogs plunged deep down when the hares approached.
At that, one hare addressed the others:
"Fellow-hares," he said. "Observe!
Those fearful frogs we saw should teach us all
That we are now pursuing folly when we look for new security,
Abandoning our well-known haunts.
We'll find no place on earth that's free of fear.
Let's all go back!"
Then all the hares returned to their own country.

No place is free of fear, toil or sorrow. Stay at home.

THE STAG

A thirsty stag was drinking
When he saw his horns reflected in the water.
He thought then to himself:
"I am the finest creature in the world!
No other beast has horns of such magnificence."
Entranced by his own image and with contemplation of his horns,
He was surprised by hounds.
They came in hot pursuit of him, their pack-master bugling after.
They harried him and sought him out,
While he in fright rushed headlong to the woods.
There, tangled by his horns, he stuck fast in the bushes.
His pursuers fell upon him.
The stag could do no more than tell himself this truth:
We love what we should scorn if we were wiser.

We love what we should scorn if we were wiser.

THE WOLF AND THE DOG

A wolf met a dog as they went running through a wood.
The wolf surveyed the dog, then said to him:
"Brother, you're very handsome, and your coat shines just like silk!"
Dog replied: "It's true. For I eat well and I have food in plenty.
I lie at leisure on a rainy day,
And then daily at my master's feet I gnaw at meaty bones.
That's how I am both sleek and fat.
If you will come with me and will obey him just as I do,
You will have more food than you could wish."
"Agreed!" said Wolf. And so they left in company together.
Before they got to town, however, Wolf perceived how the dog wore a collar,
And he saw its trailing chain.
"Brother," he said, "I see the strangest sight around your neck!
Whatever is it?"
                    "That's my chain. That chain ties me all week,
For often I would bite and savage things my master must protect.
That's why he keeps me chained.
At night I prowl the house, protecting it from thieves."
"What?" said the wolf. "You mean you cannot run at your free will?
You stay, *I'll* go! I'll never choose a chain!
I choose — while I still have the choice —
To be a wolf and roam at'large.
I do not want to live enchained in luxury.
Go to the town! I'm going to the woods."

The wolf's and the dog's friendship was thus severed by a chain.

THE LAMB AND THE GOAT

A mother-ewe gave birth.
Her shepherd took away the lamb.
He gave it to a mother-goat
Who led it to the woods, fed it, and raised it.
But when at last she saw the lamb was grown,
She called it to her, saying:
"Go, Lamb! I've kept you here too long.
You now must find your mother and your father."
But Lamb then answered wisely: "No!
It seems to me my mother is the one who fed me,
Not the one who bore me and then let me go away."

My mother is the one who fed me.

THE LION AND THE ASS

An ass met a proud lion and made salutation thus:
"God save you, brother! Yes, God save you!"
Proud Lion thought the ass behaved too boldly,
And he answered quickly:
"Since when were we so close and so familiar?"
The ass said: "What surprising things you say!
You never have regard for other beasts.
You think — quite wrongly — there is none to equal you.
Come now with me up on that hilltop.
The animals are gathered.
I'll show you how they'll fear the ass
Just as they fear THE LION."
The lion climbed the hill with him.
They stood above the valley, all the beasts below them.
The ass then started screaming, and his brays were horrible.
The animals below them fled in terror, one and all.
The ass said: "See, friend! Things turned out
Exactly as I promised!"
To that the lion answered:
"It was not your great dignity or worth — for you have neither!
It was the frightful braying that you made.
My subjects thought you were the Devil."

The fool shouts loudly, thinking to impress the world.

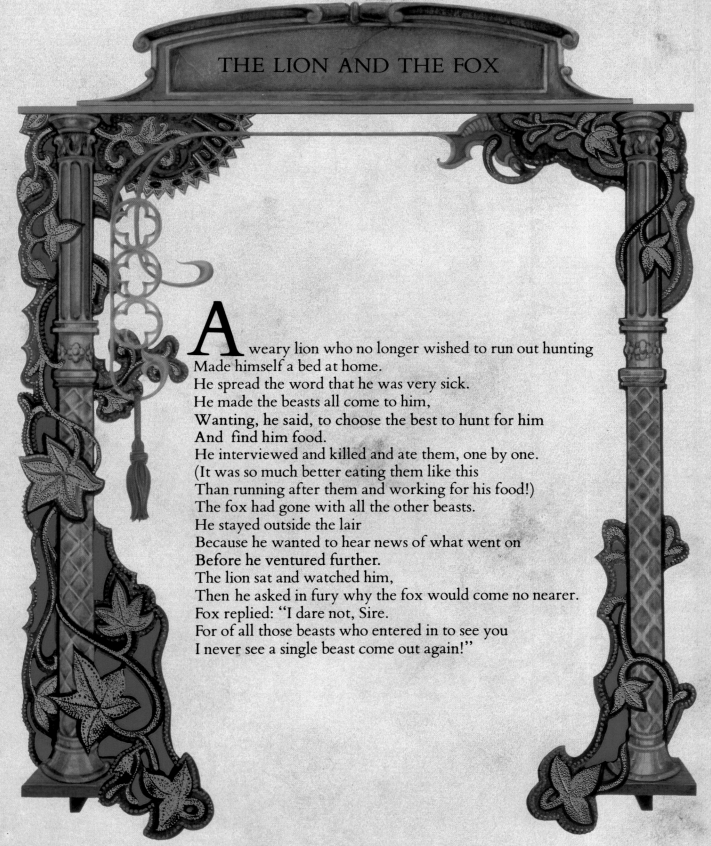

THE LION AND THE FOX

A weary lion who no longer wished to run out hunting
Made himself a bed at home.
He spread the word that he was very sick.
He made the beasts all come to him,
Wanting, he said, to choose the best to hunt for him
And find him food.
He interviewed and killed and ate them, one by one.
(It was so much better eating them like this
Than running after them and working for his food!)
The fox had gone with all the other beasts.
He stayed outside the lair
Because he wanted to hear news of what went on
Before he ventured further.
The lion sat and watched him,
Then he asked in fury why the fox would come no nearer.
Fox replied: "I dare not, Sire.
For of all those beasts who entered in to see you
I never see a single beast come out again!"

Be wary to approach the seat of power.

THE FLEA AND THE CAMEL

A flea climbed on a camel's back
And rode it all the way into a foreign land.
Then Flea, remembering his manners,
Thanked the camel who had carried him
So cosily between his camel-hairs.
"I never could have travelled on my own," said Flea.
To show my gratitude I'd gladly serve you if I could!"
But Camel answered him: "Poor Flea, you were no bother!
I did not feel your presence,
And you never burdened me."

The rich are never threatened by the poor — they do not notice them.

THE ANT AND THE CRICKET

A cricket in the winter season came upon an ant-hill
And he wandered in.
He asked for food.
He needed food, he said, because his lodgings were all bare.
The ant said: "What then did you do last Summer
During those long August days?
You should have made provision for your needs!"
"I sang," said Cricket, "and I pleased the other creatures.
But now I find not one of them is willing to repay me.
So I stopped in here."
The ant said, "Don't try singing now to me!
Better, in faith, to stock up food in Summer
Than to come begging at ants' doors,
Shivering to death!
Why should I give you food?
You can't give help to *me*!"

Each must diligently take thought for his own livelihood.

THE PEASANT, THE WIFE AND THE LOVER

A peasant, passing by his house, looked in
And saw a man upon the bed beside his wife.
"Alas," he moaned, "What did I see?"
"What *do* you see, fair lord?" his wife replied.
"I thought I saw a man who held you in his arms
And kissed you on my bed!"
The wife got vexed and said: "Now there you go again!
You have, without a doubt, a crazy habit of confusing true and false."
"I saw it," he replied. "I must believe it!"
"You fool," she said, "to think that all you've seen is true!"
To prove her point she took him to a bowl of water,
Made him peer into its depths.
"What do you see in there?" she asked.
"I see myself in there," the peasant said.
"And yet," she said, "you're *not* inside that bowl with all your clothes on,
Even though you see an image of yourself in there!
Don't trust your eyes, they lie too often."
"I repent," said he.
"Each man is better off believing what his wife tells him is true
Than trusting what his own eyes wickedly behold—
They fool him with appearances."

A quick wit solves a nasty situation.

50

THE PEASANT'S PRAYER

A peasant went to church to pray.
Before he entered, he tied up his horse,
Which he loved dearly,
To a post outside the church.
He prayed to God to give him
One more horse just like the one he had.
While he made this prayer
Thieves stole his horse.
So when the peasant came out of the church,
He found his horse was gone.
The peasant then went back to church in haste.
But now he prayed devoutly
That the Lord grant him one thing:
No *second* horse which now would never please him,
But his own dear horse,
The best horse in the world for him!

Guard what you have, and do not pray beyond your needs.

53

THE FOX AND THE MOON'S SHADOW

One night a fox had gone out on the prowl
Looking for sport and amusement.
He traversed a pond,
Looked into its depths,
And there saw the moon reflected.
"*What* was that? What was *that*?" he thought.
Was there one huge cheese in the water?
If that water were less, he could get at the cheese.
Fox started to lap up the water.
He drank and he drank.
He drank till he burst!
Fox never got up from the water.

Greed brings its just reward.

THE WOLF AND THE CROW

A wolf caught sight of a crow
Who was perching on a sheep's back.
Wolf said high-handedly:
"I now see surprising things!
A crow upon Sheep's back!
Crow sits where he sits.
Crow says what he says.
Crow does what he does.
And nobody prevents him.
Crow fears no harm from any beast.
But what if *I* sat there?
Then I know well that all would scream at me
For bad intentions.
And because I wanted Sheep,
They'd never let me near her!"

The trickster rages that the trustworthy is trusted.

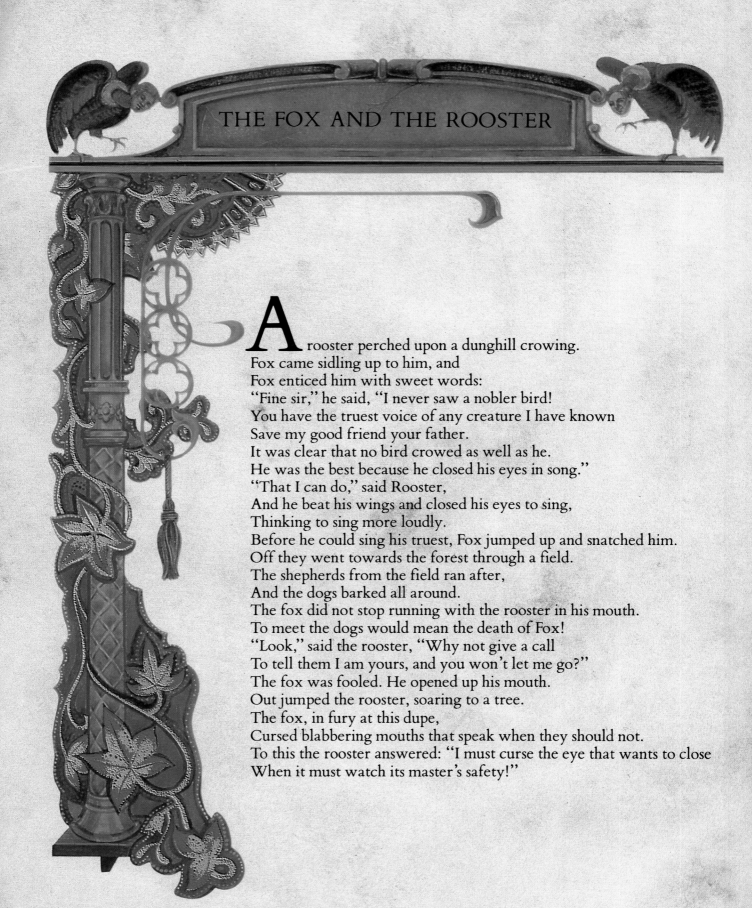

THE FOX AND THE ROOSTER

A rooster perched upon a dunghill crowing.
Fox came sidling up to him, and
Fox enticed him with sweet words:
"Fine sir," he said, "I never saw a nobler bird!
You have the truest voice of any creature I have known
Save my good friend your father.
It was clear that no bird crowed as well as he.
He was the best because he closed his eyes in song."
"That I can do," said Rooster,
And he beat his wings and closed his eyes to sing,
Thinking to sing more loudly.
Before he could sing his truest, Fox jumped up and snatched him.
Off they went towards the forest through a field.
The shepherds from the field ran after,
And the dogs barked all around.
The fox did not stop running with the rooster in his mouth.
To meet the dogs would mean the death of Fox!
"Look," said the rooster, "Why not give a call
To tell them I am yours, and you won't let me go?"
The fox was fooled. He opened up his mouth.
Out jumped the rooster, soaring to a tree.
The fox, in fury at this dupe,
Cursed blabbering mouths that speak when they should not.
To this the rooster answered: "I must curse the eye that wants to close
When it must watch its master's safety!"

Fools speak out when they should be silent, and are silent when they should speak out.

THE HORSE AND THE HEDGE

A horse saw green grass growing in a meadow.
He did not see the thorns that grew around it,
So his eager rush for food
Impaled him on a hedge of spikes.

Desire can blind us to the hazards of our enterprises.

THE CROW WHO FOUND THE PEACOCK FEATHERS

A crow who was out walking
Found some plumes and feathers from Peacock.
The feathers were so elegant
That Crow, looking his black body over,
Suddenly felt the ugliest of birds.
Why did he look like Crow and not like Peacock?
And so, to change himself, the crow tore out his feathers.
Not a one was left.
Then, dressed as Peacock, Crow went off to join the peacock clan.
But crows do not fool peacocks.
Crows look and act like crows.
Crow was to them an odd and ugly bird.
They beat him with their wings.
They tried their best to kill him.
So he struggled back to Crowdom.
He intended to resume his life as Crow.
But there, too, Crow was now an odd and ugly bird.
So Crowdom attacked Crow with beating wings.
They battered, pecked and killed this unknown stranger.

Crow should have valued what he had, not wanted the impossible.

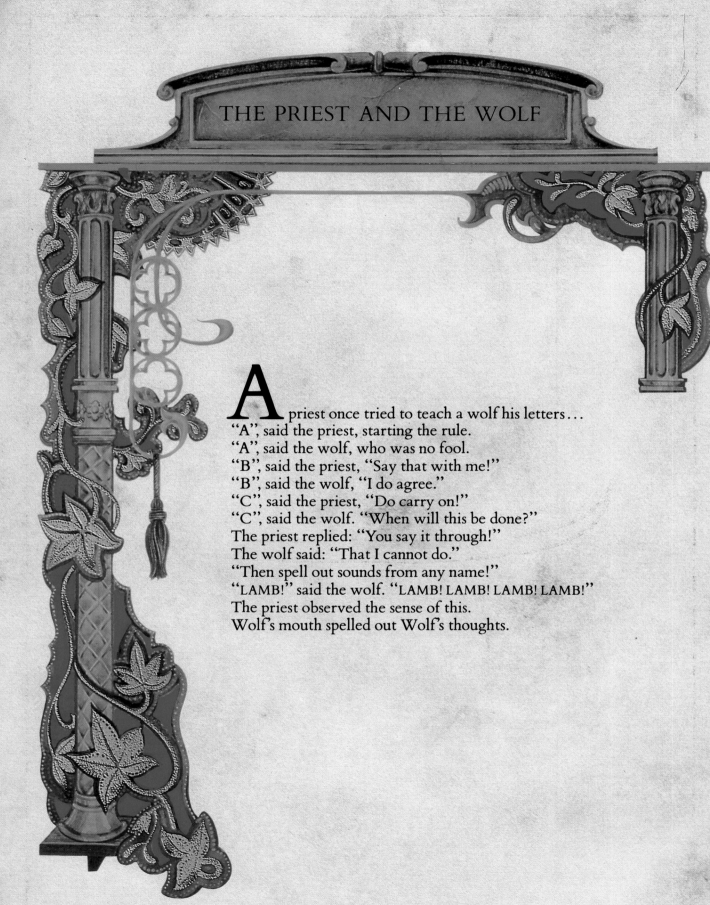

THE PRIEST AND THE WOLF

A priest once tried to teach a wolf his letters...
"A", said the priest, starting the rule.
"A", said the wolf, who was no fool.
"B", said the priest, "Say that with me!"
"B", said the wolf, "I do agree."
"C", said the priest, "Do carry on!"
"C", said the wolf. "When will this be done?"
The priest replied: "You say it through!"
The wolf said: "That I cannot do."
"Then spell out sounds from any name!"
"LAMB!" said the wolf. "LAMB! LAMB! LAMB! LAMB!"
The priest observed the sense of this.
Wolf's mouth spelled out Wolf's thoughts.

By men's words we know them.

THE BEE AND THE FLY

A bee and a fly squabbled angrily.
The fly said: "I am better far than you!
I go to places where you would not dare be seen.
I settle on the King!
All that *you* work for and accumulate
Is always taken from you.
You are thrown out of your honey-combs to die,
While I and all my friends consume your honey as we wish!"
The bee replied: "You speak the truth,
But it is obvious what a common thing you are.
In every place you go you cause annoyance.
I don't care where you go or where you sit —
That will not bring you credit!
I am loved and cherished for my good gifts."

Worthless boasters can be silenced by the truth.

THE WOLF AND THE FOX

A wolf and a fox were fighting.
They became so angry with each other,
No-one could reconcile them, make the two see reason.
Then they went before the lion.
Each there spoke his piece and told Lion the whole story.
Lion said: "In my view Fox was right and Wolf was wrong.
But, notwithstanding, there was such confusion and
Misunderstanding that,
In my view, although Wolf was obviously mistaken, yet
That lie appears more rational than the fox's truth.
I judge therefore that neither Wolf nor Fox is to be punished."

In handling grievances, opt for one side without irritating the other.

Our forefathers wrote down these fables
for our good.

Par moralité escriveient.